# A SHORT GUIDE TO IRISH ANTIQUITIES

*A stone-built ringfort at Leacanabuaile, Co. Kerry.*

# A short guide to Irish antiquities

## Sites shown on Discovery Series Ordnance Survey maps

PAUL MULLIGAN

**Word***well*

First published in 2005
Wordwell Ltd
PO Box 69, Bray, Co. Wicklow


ISBN 1869857992

British Library Cataloguing-in-Publication Data.

A catalogue record for this book is available from the British Library.

This publication has received support from the Heritage Council under the 2005 Publications Grant Scheme.

Typeset in Ireland by Wordwell Ltd

Copy-editor: Emer Condit

Printed by Castuera, Pamplona

# Contents

# ACKNOWLEDGEMENTS

I would like to thank all those who assisted me in the course of my research for this book. In particular I would like to thank the following: the ever-helpful staff in Skerries Library; Paul Walsh, who was involved in selecting the antiquities to be shown on the Discovery Series maps; Con Manning, who read through and made comments on an early draft; Eamon Cody, Claire Breen and Paddy O'Donovan, all from the National Monuments Section in the Department of the Environment, Heritage & Local Government; Paul Kerrigan for information on Martello towers.

I would also like to thank the Department of the Environment, Heritage & Local Government for providing many of the photographs for this publication, and in particular John Scarry and Con Brogan. I gratefully acknowledge the Heritage Council for their support under the Publications Grant Scheme and Ordnance Survey Ireland for permission to reproduce part of a Discovery Series map.

Finally I would like to thank Nick Maxwell and his staff at Wordwell Ltd for their work in preparing this book for publication, and my wife Ann for her help in proofreading and her support throughout the project.

All photographs are reproduced courtesy of the Department of the Environment, Heritage and Local Government, except where otherwise stated.

# Introduction

## Representation of antiquities on the Discovery Series maps

It is estimated that there are over 120,000 archaeological monuments in the state. This does not imply that there are visible remains at every site, as many have been destroyed or removed over the centuries. Ancient monuments (antiquities) are included on the Discovery Series maps only where some visible remains are still evident. Obviously, the scale of 1:50,000 imposes limitations, as does the need to avoid cluttering the map with sites, especially in built-up areas. For this reason the local or individual names of specific monuments have not been included, although many of the monuments in state care (National Monuments) are individually named.

Monuments are represented by two symbols on the Discovery Series (see sample map on page 2). A simple red dot is used for named antiquities and an open-circle symbol (also in red) is used to designate enclosures. The majority of the enclosures belong to the class of monument known as ringforts. Most of the monuments pre-date the 18th century, though a small number of sites from later periods (e.g. Martello and signal towers) have been included as sites of special interest and notable landmarks. In a number of cases more than one type of monument may be represented at a site. In this instance, attention is drawn to the principal visible monumental remains. For example, where 'Church' (or its abbreviated form 'Ch') is used, it may be assumed that, in most cases, there is a graveyard present also.

Although many of the terms used on the Discovery Series maps to describe the different monument types are self-explanatory, there are also many that require further explanation. The aim of this guide is to clarify these terms for map-users, and in so doing to increase awareness and understanding of Irish field monuments. The chronological periods and ages referred to in the guide relate to those given in the time chart on page 3.

# SAMPLE OF A DISCOVERY SERIES MAP

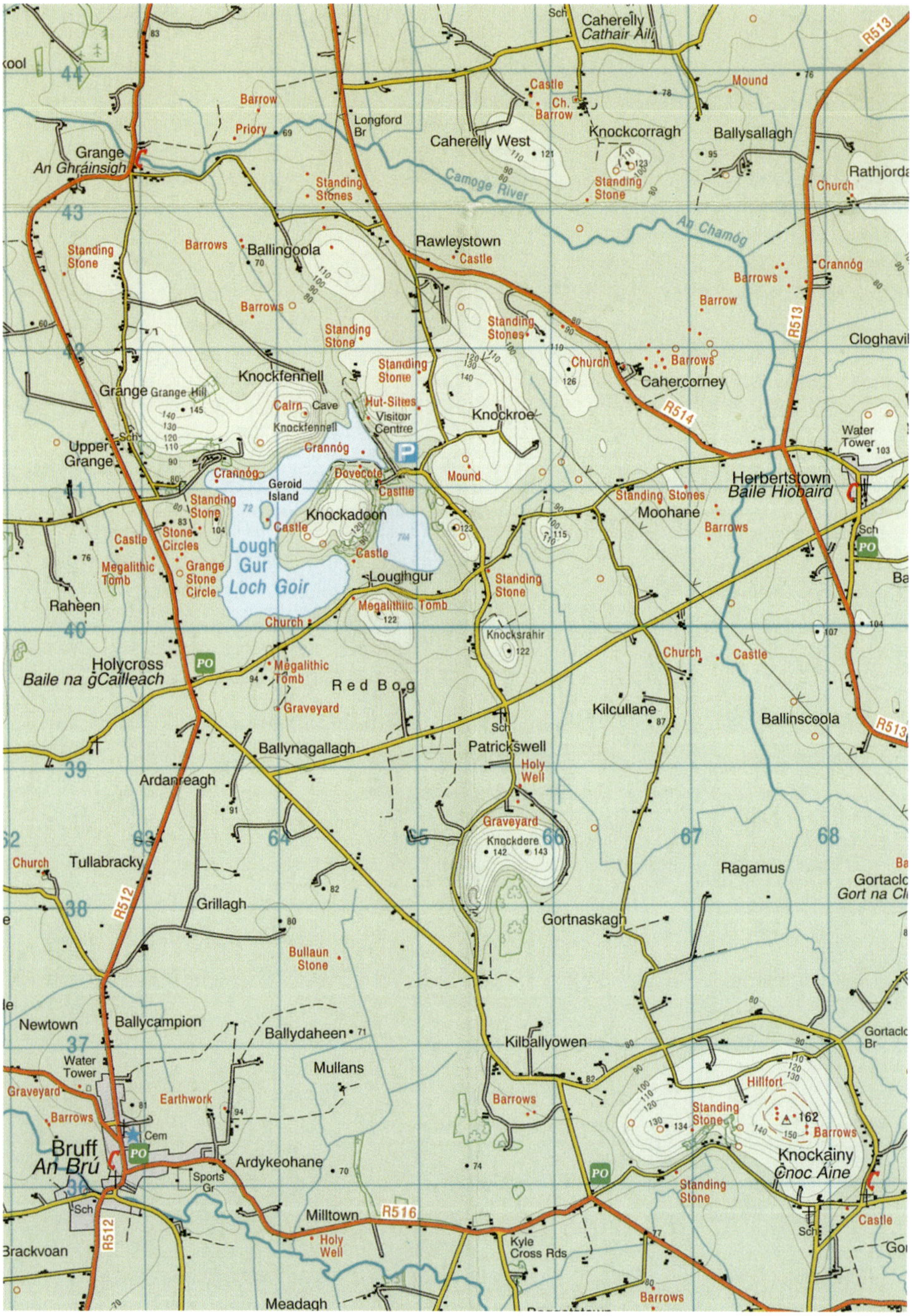


*This example from County Limerick (part of sheet 65) shows a wide variety of antiquities.*
*© Ordnance Survey Ireland and Government of Ireland (Permit No. 8100).*

# Irish Archaeological Time Chart

| | APPROXIMATE DATES | ARCHAEOLOGICAL PERIODS | SIGNIFICANT EVENTS | TYPICAL FIELD MONUMENTS |
|---|---|---|---|---|
| HISTORIC | Post-1700 | Modern (18th–21st century) | 1799–1815: Napoleonic Wars in Europe | Martello tower, signal tower |
| | AD 1550–1700 | Post-medieval (16th–17th century) | 1609–10: Plantation of Ulster | Star-shaped fort, fortified house |
| | AD 1400–1550 | Late medieval (15th–16th century) | 1536–40: Dissolution of the monasteries | Tower house |
| | AD 1150–1400 | Medieval (12th–14th century) | 1167: Arrival of the Anglo-Normans | Abbey, castle, moated site, motte and bailey, ringwork |
| | AD 400–1150 | Early medieval/Early Christian (5th–12th century)/(5th–9th century) | 795: First Viking raid. 5th century: St Patrick's mission | High cross, round tower, cross-pillar, cross-slab, ringfort, souterrain |
| PREHISTORIC | 600 BC–AD 400 | Iron Age | Beginning of ironworking | Promontory fort |
| | 2400–600 BC | Bronze Age | Introduction of metallurgy | Boulder-burial, *fulacht fia*, stone circle, stone row, cist |
| | 4000–2400 BC | Neolithic (New Stone Age) | Introduction of agriculture | Rock art, megalithic tomb |
| | 7000–4000 BC | Mesolithic (Middle Stone Age) | Earliest known phase of human settlement | Midden |

# Guide to antiquities

## ABBEY

Age range: Medieval–late medieval

An abbey is a religious house, inhabited by a community of monks and governed by an abbot. The term 'abbey' has been used in Ireland for a monastic settlement since the 6th century, but with the arrival of the Continental monastic orders, especially the Cistercians in the 12th century, the terms 'abbey' and 'abbot' acquired a new lease of life. Mellifont Abbey, Co. Louth, founded in 1142, was the first Cistercian monastery to be established in Ireland. In all, the Cistercians established a total of 36 houses in Ireland in medieval times, including Jerpoint Abbey (Co. Kilkenny), Boyle Abbey (Co. Roscommon) and Holy Cross Abbey (Co. Tipperary). *See also* **Friary**, **Monastic site**, **Priory**.

*Boyle Abbey, Boyle, Co. Roscommon. This Cistercian monastery, founded in the 12th century, reflects the change in architectural style from Romanesque to Gothic in its 60-year building history (1160–1220).*

## ANCIENT FIELD SYSTEM

AGE RANGE: NEOLITHIC–POST-MEDIEVAL

Remnants of large stone-walled rectangular fields survive in some upland areas, beyond the present extent of cultivated land. Continuous boundaries indicate that animal husbandry was practised as well as cereal cultivation. Field systems that survive in more low-lying areas tend to be smaller and can be much more irregular in form. Evidence of ancient land division has survived in many parts of Ireland, particularly in upland areas. The Céide Fields, Ballycastle, Co. Mayo, provide an example of an extensive ancient field system, dating back to the Neolithic, which was preserved under blanket bog.

## BARRACKS

AGE RANGE: POST-MEDIEVAL–MODERN (MAINLY LATE 17TH–EARLY 19TH CENTURY)

Barracks are large buildings or groups of buildings used to accommodate military personnel. During the last decade of the 17th century and the first decade of the 18th century a network of barracks was constructed across Ireland, which helped to consolidate English rule at that time. They were sited for the most part in important towns, while smaller, defensible barracks or redoubts were built in more isolated areas at strategic locations, such as mountain passes and river crossings. A high perimeter wall, usually without any particular defensive features, enclosed the more numerous cavalry and infantry barracks. During the 18th century new barracks for cavalry and infantry were built from time to time, in some cases replacing earlier

*Millmount Barracks, Drogheda, Co. Louth, constructed by the British in 1808. The building on the right, which was the officers' mess of the former military complex, now houses the Millmount Museum. (Photo: P. Mulligan)*

*Small ring-barrow at Cooga, Co. Tipperary.*

ones. The threat of an invasion of Ireland during the Napoleonic Wars (1799–1815) stimulated the construction, by the British, of large barracks. These new barracks were provided with defensible perimeter walls with musket-loops, and particular attention was paid to defence of the gateways. Among the earliest barracks constructed in Ireland were those at Athlone in 1697, Cork in 1698 and Ballyshannon in 1700. Millmount Barracks, Drogheda, Co. Louth, constructed in 1808, is an example of a barracks built during the Napoleonic era.

## BARROW/BARROW CEMETERY

AGE RANGE: NEOLITHIC–IRON AGE (MAINLY IRON AGE)

A barrow is an earthen burial mound like a tumulus, but it also has outer features such as a ditch and outer bank. There are various forms of barrow, the most common being a ring-barrow. Ring-barrows are circular mounds of earth, usually quite low, surrounded by a ditch with an external bank. Some have an entrance through the bank and a corresponding causeway across the ditch. A small number of elaborate ring-barrows have multiple banks and ditches. Most ring-barrows range in overall diameter from 15m to 25m, with a few very large ones exceeding 30m. On excavation, barrows have been found to contain cist or pit burials or simple pockets of cremated remains. Evidence of crouched and extended unburnt burials has also been found in ring-barrows. It is believed that the emergence of the rite of unburnt burial in the early centuries AD reflects the influence of contacts with Roman Britain at that time. Barrows are widely distributed throughout the country and they occasionally occur in groups or cemeteries, as for example at the Curragh, Co. Kildare. *See also* **Tumulus.**

*Battery on Dalkey Island, Co. Dublin, looking out across Killiney Bay. Note the traversing platforms on which the guns were mounted. (Photo: Jason Bolton)*

## BATTERY

AGE RANGE: MODERN (EARLY 19TH CENTURY)

A battery is a general term for an emplacement or platform for artillery guns. For example, on Whiddy Island, Bantry Bay, Co. Cork, batteries were built about 1806–7 on three hilltops on the island, with deep, rock-cut ditches encircling each site. The battery guns were 24-pounders mounted on traversing platforms, spaced at regular intervals around defensible barracks. Firing over a broad parapet, each gun could be trained through about 180 degrees. The positioning of these guns on high ground ensured an extensive all-round field of fire for the artillery of each garrison. In addition to allowing for defence of Whiddy Island itself, the disposition of these fortifications defended the channels leading to the mainland anchorage, east of the island. Any vessels attempting to sail through the northern or southern channels would have been within range of the 24-pound iron shot from the guns.

## BAWN

AGE RANGE: MEDIEVAL–POST-MEDIEVAL (MAINLY 15TH–17TH CENTURY)

A bawn is a defended walled courtyard or enclosure, sometimes with corner towers for extra defence. It usually surrounds, or is attached to, a tower house or fortified house and is equivalent to the bailey in a medieval castle. The bawn wall provided protection for cattle at night and was a further line of defence for tower and fortified houses. Examples of bawns associated with tower houses are common: for example, Doe Castle, Co. Donegal, is surrounded by a turreted bawn built early in the 16th century. *See also* **Tower house**, **Fortified house**.

*Large rectangular bawn at Rathcline, Co. Longford. The remains of a 16th-century tower house and a three-storey fortified house can be seen in the north-east corner of the bawn.*

*A pair of boulder-burials and a standing stone (right foreground), Derrynamucklagh townland, Co. Kerry. (Photo: Connie Murphy)*

## BOULDER-BURIAL

AGE RANGE: BRONZE AGE (MAINLY 1500–800 BC)

A boulder-burial consists of a single large coverstone or boulder, resting on three or more much smaller supporting stones. These supporting stones are usually very low and flat-topped, seldom protruding more than 0.25m above ground level. Some boulder-burials have been found to cover a pit containing fragments of cremated bone, and from this it has been inferred that these monuments were built as memorials over formal or token burial deposits. Unlike megalithic tombs, boulder-burials were not covered by cairns or mounds and the supporting stones rarely formed a recognisable burial chamber. Over 80 boulder-burials are known in Ireland, the vast majority in counties Cork and Kerry. They usually occur alone but occasionally are found in pairs or clusters. They are also sometimes associated with other ceremonial monuments, such as stone circles, stone rows or standing stones. In the Kenmare/Bantry region, ten stone circles enclose one or more boulder-burials, while a further three occur adjacent to boulder-burials. *See also* **Megalithic tomb**.

## BULLAUN STONE

AGE RANGE: EARLY MEDIEVAL

A bullaun stone is a large boulder with one or more artificial basin-like depressions on its upper surface. The hollowed-out cavities were possibly used as mortars for grinding grain, ore or other substances. Others believe that bullaun stones held water for use in baptisms, blessings and healings ('wart wells'). They are a frequent feature of early ecclesiastical sites.

*Bullaun stone at Derrintinny, Co. Cavan.*

## CAIRN

AGE RANGE: NEOLITHIC–MODERN (MAINLY NEOLITHIC–BRONZE AGE)

Cairns are heaps or mounds, predominantly of stone, placed over and around ancient burial sites, though many may have had a purely symbolic function. For instance, they were used to cover megalithic tombs of the Neolithic Age or to cover cist graves or pit burials of the early Bronze Age. Some are more elaborate than a simple stone mound. Ring-cairns, for example, usually take the form of a low ring of stone spread around a flat interior with one opening. Sometimes there may be a small cairn in the centre, or the ring may have a kerb of small stones either on the inside or the outside. Cairn circles are small cairns (approx. 5m in diameter) delimited by low kerbstones. Cairns are frequently located on mountaintops, hilltops and ridges. A notable example is Queen Maeve's Cairn, Knocknarea, Co. Sligo. *See also* **Megalithic tomb**.

*Queen Maeve's Cairn, Knocknarea, Co. Sligo. This very large cairn, with a diameter of some 60m and a height of around 10m, is likely to contain a passage tomb.*

## CASHEL see RINGFORT

## CASTLE

AGE RANGE: MEDIEVAL–POST-MEDIEVAL (TOWER HOUSES WERE BUILT IN THE LATE MEDIEVAL AND POST-MEDIEVAL PERIODS)

The great period of castle-building in Ireland was from about 1175 to 1310. The Anglo-Norman stone fortresses of that time were built to dominate and intimidate. Some were very large indeed and consisted of a great tower (keep) standing in a courtyard (bailey) enclosed by a high defensive wall (curtain wall). Sometimes the

*Aerial view of Trim Castle, Co. Meath, the largest and earliest Anglo-Norman castle in Ireland.*

keep was defended by outer and inner curtain walls, and the outer wall was always protected by a moat, which was usually filled with water. The moat was often cut out of bedrock, which provided a ready source of stone for building the castle. Extra defence was provided by fortified towers in the curtain wall and by a large gatehouse or gateway, complete with portcullis and drawbridge. Other defensive features included indented parapets (battlements) crowning the main walls of the keep and curtain wall, and an outward slope at the foot of the external walls (base-batter). The base-batter added strength to the structure of the wall and allowed missiles, dropped down from the battlements, to be deflected outwards against attackers. The keep was the last place of refuge should the curtain wall of the castle be breached, and it also acted as the main residence of the lord, his family and his knights. Most of the servants and soldiers would have occupied wooden buildings within the bailey. For defensive reasons the keep was normally entered through a door at first-floor level, where the great hall was also situated. Large castles did not always have a keep; in fact in Ireland we have relatively few keeps. Living quarters were often within the towers of the gateway and the curtain wall. Fine examples of medieval castles with keeps are Trim Castle (Co. Meath), Carrickfergus Castle (Co. Antrim) and Adare Castle (Co. Limerick). Examples of Norman castles without keeps are Dublin Castle, Kilkenny Castle, Roscommon Castle and King John's Castle (Limerick). The beginning of the 14th century marked the end of the building of large Anglo-Norman fortresses. When castle-building resumed on a large scale in the 15th century, the predominant form was the tower house. Tower houses were fortified private residences rather than military fortifications and were erected by both Anglo-Norman and Gaelic families during the period from about 1400 to 1650. Tower houses, which are far more numerous than medieval castles, are also represented on the Discovery Series maps by the term 'Castle'. *See also* **Gatehouse**, **Tower house**.

## CATHEDRAL

AGE RANGE: MEDIEVAL–MODERN

A cathedral is the principal church of a diocese, with a bishop's throne. Following 12th-century reforms, the church in Ireland was reorganised into dioceses ruled by bishops. The first medieval purpose-built cathedrals in Ireland were built in the round-arched Romanesque style. Very little remains of these Romanesque cathedrals, as most of them were totally demolished to make way for 13th-century successors, which were generally built in the Gothic style. Examples of medieval Gothic cathedrals include St Canice's Cathedral (Kilkenny), Christ Church Cathedral (Dublin), Ardfert Cathedral (Co. Kerry) and St Mary's Cathedral (Limerick).

*Ardfert Cathedral, Co. Kerry. This 13th-century cathedral retains sections of a 12th-century Romanesque doorway and blind arcade on the west wall. An aisle and transept were added to the south side of the nave in the 15th century.*

## CHAMBERED GRAVE see MEGALITHIC TOMB

## CHURCH (often abbreviated to 'Ch')

AGE RANGE: EARLY MEDIEVAL–MODERN

The earliest Irish churches were of timber or other perishable materials, and it is only in the late 8th and 9th centuries that we first find references to stone churches. The oldest stone churches to survive are simple rectangular buildings of varying dimensions, but often measuring less than 5m long internally. They frequently incorporate very large blocks of stone in the lower courses of the walls. A common feature of these buildings was a high, steeply pitched roof, which was carried right over the gables to have its ends supported on projecting portions of the side walls, known as antae, or on corbels projecting from the corners. The sole doorway, centred invariably in the west gable wall, was typically a flat-topped, lintelled opening, wider at the base than at the top. Up until the beginning of the 12th century churches generally consisted of a simple rectangular nave, but after that time it became common for churches to have a nave and chancel, with a chancel arch separating the two. With the arrival of the round-arched Romanesque style in the second quarter of the 12th century, stone carving was extensively used for the first time in church

*Early medieval church at Labbamolaga, Co. Cork. This small church, with antae and flat-headed doorway, is on the site of a monastery founded by St Molaga in the 7th century.*

*Medieval parish church with bellcote at Kilmolash, Co. Waterford.*

architecture. In contrast to the flat lintels used in the Early Christian churches, Irish Romanesque-style churches are distinguished by round-headed doorways, windows and chancel arches decorated with a rich variety of carved designs. The Cistercian order is credited with the introduction of the pointed-arched Gothic style to Ireland, and it became the dominant style of church architecture from about the end of the 12th century until the dissolution of the monasteries in the mid-16th century. Good examples of Early Christian churches can be seen at Ardagh (St Mel's Church), Co. Longford, at Clonamery, Co. Kilkenny, at Labbamolaga, Co. Cork, and at Tuamgraney, Co. Clare. Irish Romanesque churches are found throughout the country, but the finest surviving example of this style of architecture can be seen at Cormac's Chapel, Cashel, Co. Tipperary. A good example of a late medieval Gothic-style church can be seen at Killeen, Co. Meath, which was built in the 15th century. *See also* **Oratory**.

## *CILLÍN*

AGE RANGE: MEDIEVAL–MODERN

A *cillín* or killeen is a place where unbaptised or stillborn children were buried. Also interred in *cillíní* were adults who were marginalised as regards their status in life or manner of death, including strangers or those who had committed suicide. These burial grounds are small and inconspicuous, sometimes enclosed by a low bank or wall. The graves, if marked, are generally indicated by simple low upright stones or slabs, almost invariably without any inscription. *Cillíní* are generally located in abandoned church sites or in areas of unconsecrated ground and are more common in western counties, especially County Clare. The Second Vatican Council, held in 1962, allowed consecrated ground to be used for the unbaptised.

## CIST

AGE RANGE: NEOLITHIC–IRON AGE (MAINLY BRONZE AGE)

A cist or cisted grave is a stone-lined grave containing one or more cremated or unburnt burials. They are usually constructed in underground pits and covered with a single capstone, but some cists have two or three capstones. The term also applies to stone box-like structures erected above ground and enclosed in a cairn or mound. The burial rite in the earlier part of the early Bronze Age was inhumation, but as time passed cremation became dominant, continuing until the later part of the Iron Age, when inhumation began to return under late Roman and Christian influence. The earliest inhumations were crouched or flexed and were placed in cists barely large enough to contain them. These burials were often accompanied by distinctive pottery of the food vessel variety. When cremation became dominant the remains were contained in cinerary urns. Neolithic cists occur only in the southern part of the country. Bronze Age cists are more widespread but tend to occur more in the east of the country.

*A cist at Liscooley, Co. Donegal. The remains of a crouched burial can be seen within the cist.*

## *CLOCHÁN* (pl. *CLOCHÁIN*)

AGE RANGE: PREHISTORIC–MODERN

A *clochán*, also known as a beehive hut or cell, is a circular stone structure, built without mortar on the corbel principle. Fine examples can be seen at the well-preserved, possibly 9th-century island monastery site of Skellig Michael, off the Kerry coast. Here the beehive huts, which have an almost square interior, were erected as dwellings by the monks. *Clocháin* or clochans, however, are not peculiar to monastic settlements, nor are they necessarily early structures. In the Dingle Peninsula, Co. Kerry, the remains of hundreds of clochans can be seen on hill slopes. Here they may have been used as normal domestic habitations or as transhumance dwellings (booley huts), and some comparatively modern versions are still in use today as outbuildings. Clochans occur along the west coast of Ireland and on the islands off it, but the vast majority are found in County Kerry. *See also* **Hut site**.

Clochán *or beehive hut on Skellig Michael, off the coast of County Kerry. The stones projecting from the roof of the hut were used to secure a covering of thatch or sods.*

*Copper-mine, Killarney, Co. Kerry.*

## COPPER-MINE

AGE RANGE: BRONZE AGE–MODERN

Prehistoric copper-mines are simple man-made caves following copper seams. Typically they can have a diameter of up to 2–3m and can be up to 20m long. A technique called fire-setting was the main method used to extract the copper-bearing rock. This method involved building a fire near the rock face and alternately heating and cooling the rock with water to induce fracturing. Stone tools, wooden wedges and animal bones were then used to pry the loosened rock apart before crushing it with stone mauls. The copper-bearing ore was then picked out by hand. The waste rock was discarded into nearby spoil-heaps, which are one of the characteristic features of these early mines. In order to get the copper metal from the ore, it was heated in a fire or oven (smelting) to break down the copper-bearing minerals into copper metal and sulphur gas. Prehistoric copper-mines are concentrated in the south-west, mainly in counties Cork and Kerry. Here the copper ore was obtained from copper-rich quartz vein deposits or from sedimentary copper beds within the Old Red Sandstone. The earliest known metal-mining site in Ireland is at Mount Gabriel, Co. Cork, where there was extensive mining of surface copper beds during the early to middle Bronze Age.

*Court tomb at Magheraghanrush or Deer Park, Co. Sligo. The tomb has a long central court, from which two burial chambers open off at one end and one chamber at the other end. The loose stones of the cairn have been robbed in this case, leaving only the larger structural stones.*

## COURT TOMB

AGE RANGE: NEOLITHIC

Court tombs (also known as 'court cairns'), together with portal tombs, are the earliest megalithic monuments to have been built in Ireland, dating mainly from about

4000–3000 BC. The most distinctive feature of court tombs is a roofless, semicircular, U-shaped or oval forecourt, set in front of a covered gallery (the burial vault). The burial gallery, originally covered by a low corbelled roof, is divided by jambs or sill-stones into two, three or four chambers. The forecourt usually occupies the broader, eastern end of a long rectangular or trapezoidal cairn. Cremation (which possibly took place in the court area) appears to have been the predominant burial rite, though inhumation also occurred. Over 400 examples are known in Ireland, and these, with a few exceptions, are confined to the northern half of the country. Fine examples can be seen at Creevykeel, Co. Sligo, and at Creggandevesky, Co. Tyrone. Some court tombs have a central court with burial chambers opening off each end. A fine example of this type can be seen at Magheraghanrush or Deer Park, Co. Sligo. Court tombs are represented on the Discovery Series maps by the term 'Megalithic Tomb'. *See also* **Megalithic tomb**.

## CRANNOG

AGE RANGE: BRONZE AGE–POST-MEDIEVAL (MAINLY EARLY MEDIEVAL)

A crannog was a defended settlement established on an artificial, or artificially enlarged, island. These sites are found mainly in the shallow areas of lakes and were used for occupation, rather like a ringfort but in a more defensible position. The island was normally made up of a base of stones and tree-trunks, layered with peat and brushwood, which formed a circular platform that rose above the water-level. The

*Crannog at Kilcorran Lough, Co. Monaghan.*

platform, generally between 20m and 30m in diameter, was often enclosed by a palisade of closely set wooden stakes around the perimeter to consolidate the structure and act as a defensive barrier. The name 'crannog' is derived from the Irish word *crann*, meaning a tree. Originally the term may have been applied to the surrounding timber palisades, the timber buildings within them or the timber foundations on which they were erected; nowadays it refers to the entire structure. Sometimes underwater stepping-stones or a timber causeway facilitated access to the crannog. It is clear from archaeological excavation that crannogs were most abundant during the early medieval period, apparently functioning as the dwellings of the more powerful and wealthy members of society. Evidence suggests that they continued to be occupied throughout the medieval period, and in some cases remained in use even up to the 17th century. Over 1,200 crannogs have been identified throughout the country, with large numbers occuring in north Connacht, the north midlands and south Ulster, along the drainage systems of the rivers Shannon and Erne and in the isolated lakes of the drumlin belt. Modern reconstructions of crannogs can be seen at the National Heritage Park, Ferrycarrig, Co. Wexford, at Craggaunowen, Co. Clare, and at the Ulster History Park, Omagh, Co. Tyrone.

## CROSS

AGE RANGE: MEDIEVAL–POST-MEDIEVAL

In the later medieval period crosses were often erected in market-places in towns, and in the late medieval and post-medieval periods they were also erected on roadsides, usually commemorating a person. Such wayside crosses, erected to commemorate deceased persons, are common in counties Meath and Westmeath, as exemplified by the Dowdall cross at Duleek, Co. Meath. This wayside cross was erected by Janet Dowdall in 1601 in memory of her late husband, William Bathe.

## CROSS-PILLAR

AGE RANGE: EARLY MEDIEVAL

A cross-pillar (or cross-inscribed pillar) is a standing stone or pillar stone inscribed with one or more crosses. It may mark the resting-place of an important person. Monoliths carved with crosses are amongst the earliest Christian sculptures to survive in Ireland. An example of a beautifully decorated cross-inscribed pillar can be seen at Reask, Dingle Peninsula, Co. Kerry.

*Duleek wayside cross erected by Janet Dowdall in 1601 in memory of her late husband, William Bathe. (Photo: P. Mulligan)*

*A cross-inscribed pillar stone at Reask, Dingle Peninsula, Co. Kerry.*

## CROSS-SLAB

AGE RANGE: EARLY MEDIEVAL–MEDIEVAL (MAINLY 8TH–12TH CENTURY)

Cross-slabs (or cross-inscribed slabs) are mainly grave-slabs inscribed with one or more crosses. The crosses carved on these flat stone slabs vary from the simple linear cross to complicated ringed and embellished crosses. Some also have an inscription

*Cross-slab from Clonmacnoise, Co. Offaly, with inscription in Irish seeking a prayer for the deceased.*

asking a prayer for the person commemorated. The inscriptions are usually in Irish, starting with the words '*Ór do*'. Cross-slabs are often associated with early ecclesiastical sites. The largest collection of these slabs can be seen at Clonmacnoise, Co. Offaly, where over 600 complete or fragmentary examples occur. Unlike at Clonmacnoise, examples of cross-slabs at Reefert Church at Glendalough, Co. Wicklow, may still be in their original locations, lying flat on graves, with other slabs

*Deserted medieval settlement at Grove, Co. Kilkenny. (Photo: Terry Barry)*

and small crosses serving as upright headstones. Not all cross-decorated slabs are associated with well-known monastic sites such as Clonmacnoise or Glendalough. Many are found at places that have little or no history attached to them.

## DESERTED SETTLEMENT

AGE RANGE: MEDIEVAL–MODERN

In the century or so following the arrival of the Anglo-Normans, many parts of eastern Ireland were colonised by large numbers of mostly English peasants. The Anglo-Norman lords encouraged these colonists to come to Ireland, as they were needed to help work their newly conquered lands, which were divided into estates known as manors. New villages were created at a number of these manorial centres, but many were subsequently abandoned during the troubles of the 14th century. These deserted settlements can occasionally survive as earthworks, representing the remains of houses, outbuildings and property boundaries arranged around a street or streets. The earthworks of deserted medieval villages are rare in Ireland, however. Often all that can be seen at these sites today are the remains of a church site, motte or castle. A good example of a deserted medieval settlement is at Newtown Jerpoint, Co. Kilkenny, which was founded around 1200 and deserted sometime in the 17th century.

*Part of a dovecote or columbarium beside the Benedictine priory at Fore, Co. Westmeath. (Photo: P. Mulligan)*

**DOVECOTE**

AGE RANGE: MEDIEVAL–POST-MEDIEVAL

A dovecote (also known as a columbarium) is a circular stone building in which doves or pigeons are housed. Dovecotes were a frequent feature of monasteries of Continental orders of monks but few have survived. The dovecote at the Augustinian priory at Ballybeg, Co. Cork, is the largest surviving example in Ireland.

**EARTHWORK**

AGE RANGE: PREHISTORIC–MODERN

Earthwork is a general term for earthen banks, ditches or mounds that cannot be closely classified because of their eroded or damaged condition or because of some anomalous feature. Many such sites occur throughout the country.

## EFFIGY

AGE RANGE: MEDIEVAL–LATE MEDIEVAL (MAINLY 13TH–16TH CENTURY)

An effigy is a stone-carved figure, usually placed on top of a tomb to represent the deceased. The earliest examples date from the early 13th century. The people commemorated usually belonged to the upper strata of society: kings, knights and their ladies, ecclesiastics, etc. By the 15th century a type of box-tomb became common, whereby the effigy of the deceased person was placed on top of a tomb whose sides were ornamented with Crucifixion scenes and figures of the Apostles and other saints. The best collection of effigies of knights and ladies (16th-century) is in St Canice's Cathedral in Kilkenny.

*William Burke effigy, Ballynakill, Co. Galway.*

## ENCLOSURE

AGE RANGE: PREHISTORIC–MODERN

This term usually refers to a circular enclosure that is still visible at ground level but is too eroded to be positively identified as a ringfort or any other monument type. Enclosures, like ringforts, are represented on the Discovery Series maps by a small red open-circle symbol, and thousands of examples occur throughout the country. Destroyed enclosures can be seen using aerial photography, especially in cereal crops that are sensitive to drought. As the crop matures, areas that lie over subsurface pits and ditches have greater reserves of moisture and take longer to ripen. When seen from the air, the circular patterns are very clear and betray the existence of a site, probably a ringfort. Such destroyed sites are not included on the Discovery Series maps, as they are not visible at ground level. *See also* **Ringfort**.

## FORTIFIED HOUSE

AGE RANGE: LATE MEDIEVAL–EARLY MODERN (MAINLY LATE 16TH–EARLY 17TH CENTURY)

Fortified houses are fortified private residences, normally rectangular in plan and usually no more than three storeys high with an attic. They are characterised by large mullioned and transomed windows above the ground floor, and high gables surmounted by massive chimney-stacks. Inside these houses there were numerous private rooms, with a large fireplace in almost every room. The narrow stone spiral stairs of the medieval castles and late medieval tower houses were abandoned and replaced by wider wooden stairs. Despite their modern appearance, these houses often retained defensive features from the tower house era, such as corner bartizans, machicolations over the doorway and gun loops. Fortified houses were erected by many of the major landowners in Ireland, mainly during the late 16th and early 17th centuries, and in some cases they replaced or were built onto pre-existing tower houses. Fine examples of early 17th-century fortified houses are Burncourt Castle (Co. Tipperary), Portumna Castle (Co. Galway) and Parke's Castle (Co. Leitrim). The latter has undergone extensive restoration and it now appears much as it did around 1610, when it was completed on the site of a 15th-century tower house. The walls of the original bawn were retained, but the tower house was demolished and its stones used to build the three-storey fortified manor. *See also* **Bawn**, **Tower house**.

*Portumna Castle, Co. Galway. This great semi-fortified house was constructed during the period 1609–18. Note the decorative battlements and the machicolation above the doorway.*

## FRIARY

AGE RANGE: MEDIEVAL–LATE MEDIEVAL (MAINLY 13TH–15TH CENTURY)

A friary is the term used for a monastery occupied by Franciscan, Carmelite, Augustinian or Dominican friars, although among some of the orders the term 'priory' was also used. These were mendicant friars who had taken vows of poverty and were dependent on alms for their survival. The typical Franciscan friary had a long church, standing on one side of the cloister garth, with the domestic buildings of the monastery arranged around the other three sides. The church was usually divided into two distinct parts: a choir for the friars and a nave for the laity, and from the 14th century this division was generally marked by a central tower. Today the most characteristic feature of Franciscan friaries is this central tower or belfry, which is typically tall and slender, resting on narrow arches, and which occurs almost halfway along the length of the church. The first foundations of the mendicant orders in Ireland tended to be located in the Norman towns, but during the 15th century most friaries were built in rural areas, particularly in the western half of the country. Well-preserved 15th-century Franciscan friaries can be seen at Rosserk (Co. Mayo), Muckross (Co. Kerry), Askeaton (Co. Limerick) and Quin (Co. Clare). *See also* **Abbey**, **Monastic site**, **Priory**.

*Franciscan friary at Rosserk, Co. Mayo. This almost intact friary dates from the mid-15th century. The slender square bell-tower is typical of friary design.*

## *FULACHT FIA* (pl. *FULACHTAÍ FIA*)

AGE RANGE: BRONZE AGE (MAINLY 1800–800 BC)

The term *fulacht fia* refers to a mound of burnt stones traditionally believed to be the remains of an ancient cooking site. A typical *fulacht fia* (archaeologists prefer to use the non-committal term 'burnt mound') is a relatively low mound of horseshoe- or crescent-shaped plan. Often small and inconspicuous, most are 1–2m high and may range in greatest dimensions from a few metres to over 20m in a few cases. They are usually sited close to fresh water, often near a stream, lake or river, or in waterlogged marshy ground. The relatively small numbers of these sites that have been scientifically excavated have revealed a trough lined with wattle, timber or stone, a low mound of heat-fractured stones (surrounding the trough on three sides), traces of fires (sometimes a formal hearth) and occasionally post-holes, suggesting transitory structures. The troughs are usually rectangular, about 2m long, 1m wide and 1m deep, and they either naturally filled with water or were filled from a nearby water source. Meat may have been cooked in the trough by being wrapped in straw and placed in the water, which was heated to boiling-point by the addition of hot stones extracted from the nearby fire. Continuous heating shattered the stones, and this heat-fractured material, when thrown out of the trough after use, together with ash and charcoal from the fire, eventually formed the surviving stone mound. There is no agreement as to what was the primary function of these sites. The fact that experiment has shown that

A fulacht fia *close to a stream at Rathlogan, Co. Kilkenny. This is a good example of a crescent-shaped mound.*

meat can be boiled in the trough does not prove that this was their main purpose. What seems clear is that they were used to prepare large quantities of boiling water. It has been argued that they could have been covered by light structures and used as saunas or sweathouses. It has also been suggested that they could have been used for washing or dyeing large quantities of cloth, or for dipping hides in hot water as part of leather preparation. Burnt mounds are the most common of all prehistoric field monuments found in Ireland, with over 6,000 examples recorded. They sometimes occur in clusters and have been identified in almost every part of the country, with a notable concentration in County Cork, where over 2,000 have been identified.

## GATEHOUSE

AGE RANGE: MEDIEVAL–POST-MEDIEVAL

A gatehouse is an entrance building or tower through which access is gained, usually to a castle, monastery or town. Timber gate structures were probably standard features of Early Christian monasteries, but the only one that has survived is the masonry gatehouse at Glendalough, Co. Wicklow. Few have survived even at medieval monasteries, though there is a fine example at Mellifont, Co. Louth. On the other hand, surviving gatehouses at medieval castles are quite common. Some are massive rectangular structures, with half-round towers projecting beyond the line of the curtain wall and with a chamber over the gateway containing the mechanism for the portcullis and the winding gear for the drawbridge. Examples of such gatehouses can be seen at Ballymote Castle (Co. Sligo), Roscommon Castle and Ballintober Castle (Co. Roscommon), and Greencastle (Co. Donegal). *See also* **Castle**.

*Fifteenth-century gatehouse at Mellifont Abbey, Co. Louth. (Photo: P. Mulligan)*

## HENGE

AGE RANGE: LATE NEOLITHIC–BRONZE AGE (MAINLY LATE NEOLITHIC)

Henges are the earliest form of earthen enclosure. They can range in size from 30m to 275m in diameter and are normally defined by a bank up to 4m high, with one or more entrances. The classic English henge is defined as a large circular area enclosed by an earthen bank and internal fosse. In most of the identified Irish examples there is no evidence of an internal fosse and the enclosing banks appear to have been constructed by scooping out earth from the interior. They are often found in groups, sometimes in association with passage tombs (as in the Boyne Valley), and are believed to have had some outdoor ritual or ceremonial function. They are found mainly in the eastern part of the country. In the Boyne Valley, Co. Meath, four henge monuments have been identified, the most impressive being at Dowth.

*Stackallen Henge, Co. Meath. A large earthen bank defines this circular enclosure, which is 104m in diameter. (Photo: Leo Swan)*

## HIGH CROSS

AGE RANGE: EARLY MEDIEVAL–MEDIEVAL (MAINLY 9TH–12TH CENTURY)

High crosses are tall, free-standing stone crosses, normally reaching up to 4–5m in height. The west cross at Monasterboice, Co. Louth, which is over 7m, is the tallest in Ireland. Many are richly sculpted with figured panels depicting biblical scenes, while others are purely decorative, being delicately engraved with geometrical ornament. High crosses, of which there are about 100 surviving examples, were erected in the precincts of Early Christian monasteries. Why they were erected is not clear as, unlike their modern imitations, ancient high crosses do not mark graves. What is clear is that they were powerful Christian symbols, many of them depicting scenes from both the Old and the New Testaments. The 'ringed' or Celtic cross is the most common form of high cross, with a circle or ring around the junction of shaft and arms and the application of figure sculpture to the body of the cross. The function of the ring was mainly to provide structural support, preventing the weighty indented arms from snapping off, but it also probably had a symbolic purpose. There are two main chronological groups of high crosses. The earlier grouping date from around the later 9th to the early 10th century and are largely found in the provinces of Leinster and Ulster. The later group of crosses are 12th-century and are found mainly in the provinces of Munster and Connacht. On the 12th-century crosses, biblical scenes retreat in favour of a large-scale figure of Christ, standing out in high relief on the head of the cross. The only other major figure represented is a bishop or an abbot connected with the monastery within which the cross stands. The inclusion of a figure of a bishop on such crosses reflects his enhanced status under the 12th-century reform and reorganisation of the Irish church. Muiredach's Cross at Monasterboice, Co. Louth, and the Cross of the Scriptures at Clonmacnoise, Co. Offaly, are both fine examples of great scriptural crosses from the later 9th and early 10th centuries. The high cross at Dysert O'Dea, Co. Clare, is a good example of a 12th-century high cross.

## HILLFORT

AGE RANGE: NEOLITHIC–EARLY MEDIEVAL (MAINLY LATE BRONZE AGE–IRON AGE)

A hillfort is a large enclosure, delineated by a stone rampart or earthen bank and outer ditch, encircling the top of a hill. Sometimes there are two or three lines of defence widely separated from each other. Hillforts tend to be irregular in outline since the defences follow the contours of the hilltop they enclose. They are much larger than ringforts, with internal diameters of 100m or more, and were intended for use by large

*The 9th- or possibly 10th-century west cross at Monasterboice, Co. Louth. At over 7m (23ft), it is the tallest in Ireland. (Photo: P. Mulligan)*

tribal groups rather than single families. Some hillforts may have been built primarily as defended settlements or as intermittently occupied places of refuge. However, the ramparts of many large hilltop enclosures appear to have been more symbolic than defensive, and these enclosures may have been used only for periodic communal gatherings or for ceremonial occasions. Over 60 hillfort sites have been identified in Ireland. One of the finest examples is at Mooghaun, Co. Clare, which is a large enclosure with three stone ramparts encompassing a total area of about 12 hectares. Although situated on a low hill about 80m above sea-level, this hillfort commands wide views of the Shannon Estuary. Other fine examples include Dún Ailinne, Co. Kildare, Rathgall, Co. Wicklow, and Garrangrena, Co. Tipperary.

*The hillfort at Rathgall, Co. Wicklow. The innermost stone enclosure is a medieval addition to the late Bronze Age hillfort.*

## HOLY WELL

AGE RANGE: EARLY MEDIEVAL–MODERN

A holy well is a Christianised well, hallowed by some memory or association with a saint. In some parts of Ireland the associated saint is still revered locally and the holy well is still resorted to for devotion and cures. Previously holy wells may have been places of pagan pilgrimage. The antiquity of any holy well is impossible to assess, but many patterns (annual religious gatherings) associated with them were suppressed in the early 19th century. Holy wells are common throughout the country and are sometimes located a short distance from an ecclesiastical site. For example, St Mobhi's holy well, at Grange, Co. Dublin, is located near the Early Christian church of St Mobhi.

*St Mobhi's holy well, Grange, Co. Dublin. The well was constructed without mortar, using rough boulders and flagstones. A bullaun stone is set into the lower part of the right-hand wall and a small cross can be seen carved into a large boulder above the well. (Photo: P. Mulligan)*

## HOUSE

AGE RANGE: 17TH CENTURY

This term, as used on the Discovery Series maps, applies to houses of 17th-century date. These were generally the houses of tenants of the major landowners and are usually small and simple in plan. An exception to this is Beaulieu House, located 4km east of Drogheda, Co. Louth. This impressive residence, originally built between 1660 and 1666, is one of the earliest remaining examples in Ireland of an unfortified house.

*Beaulieu House, Drogheda, Co. Louth. Originally built between 1660 and 1666, this is one of the earliest remaining examples in Ireland of an unfortified house. (Photo: P. Mulligan)*

## HUT SITE

AGE RANGE: PREHISTORIC–MODERN

Huts are small stone houses or shelters. The most common type is a booley hut, which is associated with transhumance, the practice of bringing cattle from lowland areas to higher pasture during summer months. Where the summer grazing was located far away from the farm settlement, family members moved with the livestock and lived for a couple of months in temporary dwellings, called booley huts. In Ireland this practice (known as booleying) appears to have been an important feature of the agricultural economy between the 16th and 18th centuries, but it is probable that some form of booleying was being practised from prehistoric times onward. Hut sites are located in upland and mountain areas; they occur in large numbers on the Dingle Peninsula, Co. Kerry, and are extensively scattered throughout the Caha Mountains and other parts of west Cork. *See also* ***Clochán***.

## *LEACHT*

AGE RANGE: EARLY MEDIEVAL

A *leacht* is a small, square, drystone platform made up of flat stones, which often has a cross-inscribed pillar or slab erected on it. Good examples can be seen on the small island of Inishmurray, off the coast of County Sligo, where a monastery was founded by St Molaise in the 6th century. On Inishmurray the *leachta* formed a circuit of sixteen 'stations', or stopping points, visited by pilgrims and locals annually on the Feast of the Assumption (15 August). The original function of these monuments in Early Christian times is not clear, but they may have been used as outdoor altars.

*A leacht, with a cross-pillar erected on it, on Inishmurray, off the coast of County Sligo.*

## LIGHTHOUSE

AGE RANGE: MEDIEVAL–MODERN

The oldest lighthouse in Ireland is Hook Head lighthouse, Co. Wexford, with a massive tower dating back to the late 12th–early 13th century. The tower, approximately 25m high and 12m in diameter, was built of local limestone and acted as a landmark by day and a fire-tower by night. The tower has three main compartments with roofs supported by square-ribbed vaulting and a spiral stone stairway, which ascends to the top of the tower through the thickness of the wall. In the 17th century a lantern to house the beacon fire was constructed on top of the tower. The glazed lantern enclosed the coal fire, shielding it from strong winds; a flue through the top conducted the smoke away from the fire, thus exhibiting a brighter light for mariners. In 1791 coal was abandoned as a source of fuel; a large new lantern was erected, and at least twelve oil lamps with reflectors installed. In the 19th century the modern lighthouse was built on top of the medieval turret. Except for a short closure in the 17th century, this unique tower has served as a lighthouse for almost eight centuries and is one of the oldest lighthouses in the world still in operation.

*Hook Head lighthouse, Co. Wexford, one of the oldest lighthouses in the world still in use today. (Photo: A. Mulligan)*

## MARTELLO TOWER

AGE RANGE: MODERN (BUILT FROM 1804 TO 1815)

Martello towers are circular gun towers, sited at prominent locations along the coast. They were erected by the British for protection against the threat of sea invasion by French forces during the Napoleonic Wars. Most of the towers are of uniform size: approximately 12m high, 10.5m in diameter and with walls about 2.4m thick. They had a simple arrangement, consisting of three floors. The ground floor contained a gunpowder and shot magazine, the first floor was used as living quarters for the soldiers, and the flat roof usually contained a single gun platform with a traversing 24-pounder cannon, mounted on a swivel. The cannon was capable of traversing 350 degrees and had a range of 1.6km. The entrance to the tower was through a doorway at first-floor level, reached by external staircase or ladder. The doorway was normally positioned on the landward side of the tower and the outside of the door was usually covered with iron sheeting. A narrow spiral staircase, inserted in the thick walls, gave access from the first floor down to the magazine and up to the gun platform. Above the door of several of these towers is a machicolation supported on corbels, projecting beyond the parapet, for defence of the entrance. The name 'Martello' was derived

*Martello tower at Drumanagh, Co. Dublin. Note machicolation above the first-floor entrance. (Photo: P. Mulligan)*

from Cape Mortella in Corsica, where a British naval force had great difficulty in dislodging Napoleonic forces from a similar tower. So impressed were the British that they enclosed details in their correspondence with the British Admiralty, but the word Mortella became corrupted to Martello, and hence the name. Napoleon never sent a navy to Ireland, and after his death the towers were evacuated. A total of 47 free-standing Martello towers were built in Ireland, of which 39 still survive. The first period of construction was from 1804 to about 1806, including twelve towers north and fourteen south of Dublin, two in County Wexford and five in Bantry Bay (four on Bear Island and one on Garinish Island). During the 1811–15 period further towers were built, including two near Duncannon Fort, Co. Wexford, five at Cork Harbour, three on Galway Bay, two on the Shannon Estuary, one on the west side of Lough Swilly (Muckamish tower) and one at the entrance to Lough Foyle (Magilligan tower). The Martello tower on Haulbowline Island in Cork Harbour is the only one in Ireland with its original cannon, mounted on a reconstructed gun carriage, still in place.

## MASS ROCK

AGE RANGE: 17TH–18TH CENTURY

During the 17th and 18th centuries the public celebration of Roman Catholic worship virtually disappeared in Ireland because of persecution and legal repression. The discriminatory penal laws, enacted from 1695 by an all-Protestant parliament in Dublin, deprived Catholics of the freedom of worship, among other things. Such liturgy as there was took place in private houses and in hidden places in the countryside, where Mass rocks were used. A Mass rock is a large, flat rock, which provided a table on which the Mass was celebrated in secret by a fugitive priest during the penal times. While the local people prayed and offered the Mass with their priest, one of the congregation kept watch for fear of a raid by soldiers. This picture represents the worst period of persecution, but even when the danger of arrest and imprisonment for clergy and their congregation had subsided, Mass rocks continued to be used, particularly in Connacht and Ulster, either because the people were too poor to build a Mass house or because the local landlord refused to give land on which they could build one. Mass rocks are often recognisable by the mark of one or more small crosses carved into the stone. They are found throughout the country, particularly in Connacht and Ulster.

*Mass rock at Ards Forest Park, Ards Peninsula, Co. Donegal. (Photo: P. Mulligan)*

## MEGALITHIC TOMB/MEGALITHIC CEMETERY

AGE RANGE: NEOLITHIC–EARLY BRONZE AGE (MAINLY NEOLITHIC)

A megalithic tomb is a burial chamber, or chambers, built of large unhewn stones known as megaliths. Originally enclosed within a cairn of stones or a mound of earth, the chambers were accessible through an entrance. Frequently the covering cairn or mound has been removed, leaving only the ruined chamber, variously referred to as a 'dolmen', 'cromlech', 'giant's grave', 'druid's altar' or 'Diarmuid and Gráinne's bed'. These tombs were constructed by settled farming communities and used for collective burial during the Neolithic and early Bronze Age periods. The remains interred therein were accompanied by grave-goods, including stone implements and pottery vessels. Evidence recovered suggests that cremation was the usual burial rite. Sometimes tombs constructed in the Neolithic period were reused for burial during the early Bronze Age. These later burials (with accompanying grave-goods) were placed in the chamber of the tomb or inserted into the cairn. Over 1,500 megalithic tombs have been identified in Ireland and most of these monuments can be assigned to one of four major categories, each named after an important distinguishing feature:

court tombs—open forecourt in front of tomb entrance;
portal tombs—entrance to chamber flanked by two tall portal stones;
passage tombs—narrow passage leading to burial chamber;
wedge tombs—wedge-shaped burial chamber.

Passage tombs are often grouped together in cemeteries, as at Carrowmore and Carrowkeel, Co. Sligo, and at Brú na Bóinne (Boyne Valley) and Loughcrew, Co. Meath. The most famous megalithic tomb in Ireland is the passage tomb at Newgrange, Co. Meath. On the Discoverer Map series produced by the Ordnance Survey of Northern Ireland, megalithic tombs are normally represented by the term 'Chambered Grave'. *See also* **Court tomb**, **Portal tomb**, **Passage tomb**, **Wedge tomb**.

*Aughnacliffe portal tomb, Co. Longford. The townland of Aughnacliffe (*acha na cloiche *= field of the stones) derives its name from this megalithic tomb, which dates back to the Neolithic period. (Photo: P. Mulligan)*

## MEMORIAL

AGE RANGE: POST-MEDIEVAL–MODERN

This term is used to describe wayside monuments erected from the early 17th century onwards, particularly in the west of Ireland. They usually consist of a rectangular stone pier in which a plaque commemorating one or more individuals has been set.

## MIDDEN

AGE RANGE: MESOLITHIC–MEDIEVAL

A midden is a rubbish-heap or refuse-dump composed of the discarded remains of human food debris. They are usually found in coastal areas, close to the high-tide mark, and are largely made up of accumulated shellfish remains. The shellfish represented at such sites include oysters, cockles, mussels, clams, winkles and limpets. In addition to shells, middens normally contain charcoal and burnt stones, and may also contain fragments of fish or animal bone, artefacts and the remains of hearths. Though often associated with the Mesolithic period, most of the shell middens known in Ireland belong to later periods.

*Small shell midden at Dooey, Co. Donegal.*

## MOATED SITE

AGE RANGE: MEDIEVAL (MAINLY LATE 13TH–EARLY 14TH CENTURY)

A moated site is a square or rectangular enclosure, defined by a wide moat. The moat could be 2–10m or more in width and was usually designed to hold water, unlike the fosses of other earthworks. The upcast material from the moat was spread on the interior to give a raised platform, on average 30m across, and to enclose it with a defensive bank. Originally a wooden palisade would have surmounted the bank. The interior would have contained a dwelling-house and other farm buildings, usually built of wood. Moated sites were normally the settlements of lesser Anglo-Norman farmers associated with a period of secondary colonisation, from the middle of the 13th century. They functioned as small, defended farmsteads, just as ringforts had done in the early medieval period. About 1,000 possible moated sites have been identified, concentrated in the south and east of the country. They are not usually found closely associated with known medieval nucleated settlements. In fact they are often located in isolation from each other, in the more peripheral parts of the Anglo-Norman-controlled areas, where the colonists felt most threatened by their Irish neighbours. Not all moated sites were built by Anglo-Normans. Some sites in Connacht were built by Gaelic lords around AD 1300, the moated site at Ogulla, Co. Roscommon, being a possible example.

*Moated site at Ogulla, Co. Roscommon.*

*The monastic site at Clonmacnoise, Co. Offaly. Included within the site are the remains of six churches, a cathedral, two round towers, three high crosses and more than 600 cross-inscribed grave-slabs.*

## MONASTIC SITE

AGE RANGE: EARLY MEDIEVAL–MEDIEVAL

Monasteries are places where a community of religious live and practise their religion, and a large number were founded in Ireland, particularly in the 6th and 7th centuries. These early monasteries were built largely of wood, and even when the churches were being built in stone (from the 9th century) the domestic buildings of the monastery (situated away from the free-standing churches) would still have been constructed of wood or post-and-wattle. The later medieval monasteries, on the other hand, usually consisted of a connected complex of large masonry buildings arranged around a quadrangular cloister garth or open courtyard, with the church on one side and the domestic buildings of the monks (refectory, kitchen, dormitory etc.) on the other three sides. A feature common to almost all early monastic sites was an encircling enclosure, normally round or oval in shape, within which stood the church and monastic buildings. The enclosing element was usually a bank and fosse but sometimes it consisted of a stone wall. For example, the Early Christian monasteries at Kells, Co. Meath, and Lusk, Co. Dublin, have both left traces of their early monastic enclosures in the layout of the modern streets. From the 9th/10th century high crosses and round towers became common features of many of the more important monasteries, and in addition to being religious centres the large monasteries also became important centres of population, learning, trade and craftsmanship. There are a number of well-preserved small Early Christian monasteries along the west coast of Ireland and on the islands off it. Remarkable examples of these are at Skellig Michael, off the Kerry coast, and at Inishmurray, off the Sligo coast. The larger monasteries are spread throughout the country and are usually situated on good land or close to important routeways. Important examples of monasteries developed along main routes are at Glendalough, Co. Wicklow, and at Clonmacnoise, Co. Offaly. *See also* **Abbey**, **Friary**, **High cross**, **Priory**, **Round tower**.

## MOTTE/MOTTE AND BAILEY

AGE RANGE: MEDIEVAL (MAINLY LATE 12TH–EARLY 13TH CENTURY)

A motte is a large, steep-sided earthen mound with a flat top. Originally there was a wooden tower, surrounded by a timber palisade, on top of the mound. The material for the motte would normally have been derived from a large fosse at its base, which may now be filled in. The motte is sometimes accompanied by an attached enclosure called a bailey, which is delimited by an earthen bank and outer fosse and is usually rectangular or oval in shape. Originally the bailey was also protected by a timber palisade and was connected to the motte by a flying bridge or raised walkway. The bailey usually contained most of the important buildings and the motte acted only as a last resort, to which the inhabitants of the bailey would retreat in the event of attack.

*Motte and bailey at Knockgraffon, Co. Tipperary.*

Some of these 'earthwork castles' were built as campaign forts, but most were built as manorial centres. The owners and builders of mottes in Ireland were not exclusively from the upper social strata, but the vast majority, if not all, were Anglo-Normans. Evidence exists in Ireland for approximately 350 mottes. They occur mainly in the south and east of the country and are concentrated in the areas that were controlled by the Anglo-Normans. They were usually sited at strategically important locations or at population centres. A good example of a motte with bailey attached can be seen at Knockgraffon, Co. Tipperary. *See also* **Deserted settlement, Ringwork**.

## MOUND

AGE RANGE: PREHISTORIC–MODERN

This is a general term for an earthen mound. It is used when the site cannot be identified as a tumulus or a barrow owing to its unusual morphology, or where the location of the site might indicate a possible modern origin. Mounds are a common occurrence throughout the country.

## OGHAM STONE

AGE RANGE: IRON AGE–EARLY MEDIEVAL (MAINLY 4TH–7TH CENTURY)

Ogham stones are stones with ancient inscriptions carved on them, which represent the earliest Irish form of writing. The inscriptions commemorate individuals and provide some of their genealogy, usually in the form of 'A descendant of B'. A key to ogham script can be found in the 14th-century Book of Ballymote. It is based on the Latin alphabet, but the letters are represented by up to five strokes or notches cut along the edge of standing stones. Each inscription begins at the bottom of the stone and continues towards the top and, if necessary, continues downwards along the opposite edge of the stone. The use of ogham script in Ireland dates back to the 4th century AD, if not earlier, and it continued in use until after the 8th century, apparently straddling the transition from paganism to Christianity. Ogham stones are an early feature of some ecclesiastical sites, especially in the south of the country, as at Ardfert, Co. Kerry, and Ardmore, Co. Waterford. Some have contemporary crosses carved on them, while a few bear inscriptions that are clearly Christian in content. About 330 ogham stones have been found in Ireland, the bulk of these in counties Cork, Kerry (the Iveragh and Dingle peninsulas in particular) and Waterford. Some ogham stones may also have been used as boundary-markers, and some were reused as lintels in souterrains or other later structures.

*Ogham stone at Derrynane, Co. Kerry.*

## ORATORY

AGE RANGE: EARLY MEDIEVAL–MODERN

An oratory is a small stone church. Early medieval oratories are small rectangular structures, some of which had drystone corbelled roofs. The stone-roofed oratories, built entirely without mortar, are almost exclusively confined to County Kerry, where the most complete example is Gallarus Oratory on the Dingle Peninsula. *See also* **Church**.

*Oratory at Gallarus, Dingle Peninsula, Co. Kerry. This is the most complete example of a stone-roofed oratory built entirely without mortar.*

## PASSAGE TOMB

AGE RANGE: NEOLITHIC

A passage tomb (also known as 'passage grave') is a megalithic tomb normally consisting of a circular mound or cairn, usually delimited by a kerb or retaining wall of large stones, with a narrow passage leading from the edge of the cairn to a burial chamber within. The passage is generally built of upright stones (orthostats) and roofed with flat lintels, while the chamber is often roofed with horizontally laid overlapping courses of slabs to form a high, corbelled vault. Cremation was the predominant burial rite and the passage facilitated the repeated use of the chamber, where one or more large stone-carved basins are sometimes found. It is believed that these 'basin stones' were

*Passage tomb of Dumha na nGiall (Mound of the Hostages), on the Hill of Tara, Co. Meath.*

placed in the chamber to receive the cremated remains of the dead, together with personal ornaments, such as bone pendants, beads and bone or antler pins. A feature of passage tombs is the presence of a type of Neolithic pottery, known as Carrowkeel ware. It is generally thick, coarse and heavily gritted and the decoration is crude and extensively applied. In contrast to the pottery, an impressive feature of a number of passage tombs is the presence of carved or picked designs on many of the structural stones of the tomb or its kerb. This art is abstract in form and includes many curvilinear and angular designs. Passage tombs are often situated on ridges or hilltops (e.g. the Mound of the Hostages on the Hill of Tara) and, unlike other megalithic tombs, they are generally found in groups or cemeteries. There are four major megalithic cemeteries in Ireland: at Carrowmore and Carrowkeel in County Sligo, and at Brú na Bóinne (the Boyne Valley) and Loughcrew in County Meath. Over 230 passage tombs have been identified. Their distribution is largely concentrated in the northern and eastern parts of the country, and almost half occur within the four major cemeteries. The most famous Irish passage tomb is at Newgrange, Co. Meath. At the midwinter solstice, for a few days around 21 December the rays of the rising sun shine directly through the roof-box above the entrance, down the passage and into the tomb chamber. Passage tombs are represented on the Discovery Series maps by the term 'Megalithic Tomb' or 'Megalithic Tomb Cemetery'. *See also* **Megalithic tomb**.

## PORTAL TOMB

AGE RANGE: NEOLITHIC

A portal tomb is a megalithic tomb, usually consisting of a single short subrectangular burial chamber made up of a number of upright stones covered by one or occasionally two very large roof stones or capstones. The terms 'dolmen' and 'portal dolmen', also used to describe these monuments, derive from the Breton *daul* (table) and *maen* (stone). Usually the entrance to the tomb is flanked by a pair of tall portal stones, and sometimes a stone is set between the two portals, which hinders access or, in some cases, fully seals the entrance to the chamber. The most distinctive feature of these tombs is that they have extremely large capstones, which usually rest on the two portal stones and a back stone. The side stones of the chamber do not normally reach the capstone, and it is possible that the spaces were filled by corbelling. The massive capstones were presumably placed in position by being hauled up an earthen ramp. The Browne's Hill portal tomb in County Carlow has a granite capstone that is thought to weigh about 100 tonnes—the largest capstone of any megalithic tomb in Ireland. Of the approximately 180 portal tomb sites in Ireland most are concentrated in the northern half of the country, but they are also common in south Leinster and Waterford. Many are situated in valleys or on hillsides. This is particularly apparent in the south-east, where the tombs occur close to rivers. Fine examples of portal tombs can be seen at Kilclooney More (Co. Donegal), Poulnabrone (Co. Clare), Proleek (Co. Louth) and Legananny (Co. Down). Portal tombs are represented on the Discovery Series maps by the term 'Megalithic Tomb'. *See also* **Megalithic tomb**.

*Proleek portal tomb, Ballymascanlon, Co. Louth. Here two tall, well-matched stones, acting as a portal or doorway into the burial chamber, support, with the aid of a third upright, a massive granite capstone. (Photo: P. Mulligan)*

## PRIORY

AGE RANGE: MEDIEVAL–LATE MEDIEVAL

A priory is a religious house inhabited by a community of monks and governed by a prior. It is a common term used among some of the orders of mendicant friars. Kells Priory, Co. Kilkenny, which was founded by Augustinian monks from Cornwall in 1193, has the largest monastic enclosure in Ireland. *See also* **Abbey**, **Friary**, **Monastic site**.

*Kells Priory, Co. Kilkenny, one of the largest medieval monasteries in Ireland.*

## PROMONTORY FORT

AGE RANGE: LATE BRONZE AGE–MEDIEVAL (MAINLY IRON AGE)

Coastal promontory forts consist of the fortification of the landward side of naturally defensive sea promontories. Many cliff headlands around the coast were defended by the erection of large earthen banks or massive stone ramparts cutting off the neck of a coastal promontory. Sometimes more than one line of defence can be seen, with various combinations of earthen banks, ditches and large stone walls used. Inland promontory forts, which are far fewer in number, are located in prominent positions overlooking or projecting into lowland. Promontory forts vary greatly in size and are frequently indicated in place-names by the element *dún*. In all, about 300 examples are known, with the majority occurring along the Atlantic seaboard. Examples of coastal promontory forts include Dún Dúchathair (Inishmore, Co. Galway), Dunbeg (Dingle Peninsula, Co. Kerry) and Drumanagh (Loughshinny, Co. Dublin). A notable example of an inland promontory fort is Caherconree, Co. Kerry, which is located over 600m above sea-level in the Slieve Mish Mountains.

*Dún Dúchathair promontory fort, Inishmore, Aran Islands, Co. Galway. A massive drystone wall defends the cliff-bound promontory. The entrance was between the cliff and the wall on the left.*

## RATH see RINGFORT

## RINGFORT

AGE RANGE: EARLY MEDIEVAL (MAINLY 7TH–9TH CENTURY)

An earthen ringfort is a circular or subcircular area surrounded by one or more earthen banks and outer fosses. The majority of ringforts are enclosed by a single bank and ditch (univallate ringforts), but bivallate and, on very rare occasions, trivallate ringforts also occur. The banks (made from material dug from the ditches) normally range between 3m and 5m in width and between 0.5m and 2m in height. The diameter of ringforts varies from 15m to 60m, the average being about 33m. 'Fort' is a somewhat misleading term, as ringforts were not military fortifications. They were in fact the normal defended homesteads of the better-off farming people in Ireland during the early medieval period. A distinguishing feature of ringforts is an entrance through the bank or banks, with corresponding causeway over the fosse or fosses, which gives access to the interior. The entrance is usually in the east or south-east section of the ringfort, regardless of the aspect of the site. Originally a large timber gate might have stood at the entrance, together with a timber palisade on top of the bank for added protection. Within the enclosure the inhabitants (usually a single family group) normally lived in circular houses made of post-and-wattle or timber.

*An earthen ringfort at Lisbride, Co. Roscommon.*

*A stone-built ringfort at Leacanabuaile, Co. Kerry. The walls of stone buildings within the fort were uncovered during archaeological excavations.*

Ringfort-dwellers were mainly cattle-farmers, and there was open space within the enclosure where cattle could be penned overnight or during times of danger. Within the ringfort there may also have been specialised areas devoted to particular tasks such as ironworking, grain storage, or spinning and weaving. Underground refuges or souterrains are often found in, or associated with, ringforts. In different parts of the country earthen ringforts are also known by the terms 'rath' or '*lios*'. In some cases, especially in the west of Ireland, a massive stone rampart encloses the site in place of a bank and ditch. This type of ringfort is called a 'cashel', 'caher' or stone fort, and tends to have a smaller diameter than the earthen type. Some well-preserved stone-built examples have terraces and steps on the inner face of the rampart, as for example at Staigue Fort, Co. Kerry. Ringforts are the commonest type of antiquity in Ireland, with over 45,000 known examples. They were normally sited in good fertile areas that were able to support farming communities, and they are frequently found on the upper slopes of low hills, where they could avoid the heaviest lowland clays. The majority are located between 30m and 200m above sea-level. Stone-built ringforts are more common in western districts, where stone was more plentiful. Ringforts are represented on the Discovery Series maps by a small red open-circle symbol, though not all such symbols should be taken as referring to one. *See also* **Enclosure**, **Souterrain**.

## RINGWORK

AGE RANGE: MEDIEVAL (MAINLY LATE 12TH–EARLY 13TH CENTURY)
A ringwork is, like a motte, a defensive earthwork castle dating from the early phase of the Anglo-Norman settlement. It is an embanked circular enclosure, with an internal bank and external fosse. It had a palisade around the top of the bank, a fortified timber gate-tower and usually a wooden tower inside the enclosure. In contrast with a motte, where the major defensive element was the height of the mound, ringwork castles depended on the strength of their perimeter defences, and it is the more pronounced nature of their banks and their wider fosses that help distinguish them from the more common ringforts, which they resemble in form. The entrance to a ringwork is also distinguishable from a ringfort in that it will often have a pronounced ramp. Another characteristic feature of ringworks is their strategic siting. The Anglo-Norman invaders normally selected only strategically important locations for such fortresses. For example, a ringwork castle near Ferrycarrig, Co. Wexford, erected by the Anglo-Normans in 1169–70, is situated on a promontory overlooking the Slaney River. Recent archaeological excavations at Trim Castle, Co. Meath, Carlow Castle, Kilkenny Castle and Limerick Castle have all revealed evidence of ringworks underneath the stone buildings. *See also* **Motte and bailey**.

*Ringwork at Danestown, Co. Meath. Originally regarded as a bivallate ringfort, it consists of a raised central area, defined by the remains of an earthen bank, with an external fosse and outer bank.*

## ROCK ART

AGE RANGE: NEOLITHIC–BRONZE AGE

Rock art (also called rock carvings or petroglyphs) is the carving or picking of motifs or symbols on the surface of naturally occurring rock outcrops. It is also occasionally found on isolated boulders, on standing stones or incorporated into early Bronze Age monuments, such as on the underside of cist roof-slabs. In Ireland the motifs are generally limited to small hemispherical hollows known as cup-marks, or cup-marks enclosed by one or more concentric circles. Sometimes these circles or rings may be cut by a radial groove or line extending from the central cup-mark. Many suggestions have been put forward as to what inspired prehistoric people to leave their mark on the landscape in such a fashion, but the function and meaning of rock art is still uncertain. The majority of rock art sites have been found on lower mountain slopes, close to fresh water, usually a river or lake, and it may have been an important element in territorial control. Some of the complex sites at higher altitudes, such as at Reyfad, Co. Fermanagh, and Derrynablaha, Co. Kerry, may mark routeways or boundaries. Rock art has been recorded at over 100 sites in Ireland, with concentrations identified in the Iveragh and Dingle peninsulas of County Kerry, in west Cork, in Inishowen in north Donegal, in County Louth and in south Leinster (mainly County Carlow).

*Rock art at Kealduff Upper, Co. Kerry. (Photo: Con Manning)*

## ROUND TOWER

AGE RANGE: EARLY MEDIEVAL–MEDIEVAL (MAINLY 10TH–MID-12TH CENTURY)

Round towers are tall, slender, normally free-standing circular stone towers with conical roofs. They were built with the aid of mortar, enabling the stonemasons to attain heights in excess of 30m, making them one of the most striking features of early Irish ecclesiastical sites. The Irish word for round tower is *cloigtheacht*, meaning bell-house or belfry, and it is generally agreed that they were constructed as belfries for stone churches. In addition to this primary function, they may also have had secondary uses such as the storage of valuables and as places of refuge in times of raids. The fact that most are provided with high-level doorways, placed up to 4m above the original base of the tower, supports this theory. Round towers are a feature of many of the more important monasteries and are normally situated to the west of the principal church, with the doorway of the tower facing the church. Inside the tower there were originally up to seven (typically five or six) individual floor landings, linked by ladders and lit by occasional small windows. At the highest floor level (the bell-floor), beneath the stone cap, four larger windows are normally found, which dispersed the sound of the bell or bells. The original timber floors have all disappeared, but in a few cases modern replacements have been inserted to allow the visitor to climb to the top, for example at Devenish, Co. Fermanagh, and at St Brigid's Round Tower, Kildare town. In Ireland, over 70 round towers, in various states of preservation, have survived. Some well-preserved examples include those at Antrim, Co. Antrim, Ardmore, Co. Waterford, Clondalkin, Co. Dublin, Glendalough, Co. Wicklow, and Killala, Co. Mayo.

*Round tower, Glendalough, Co. Wicklow. round tower is one of the tallest in the co Its conical stone roof was reconstructed t the end of the 19th century.*

## SIGNAL TOWER

AGE RANGE: MODERN (BUILT 1804–6)

The British Admiralty set up a coastal signalling system in 1794 along the south and east coasts of England and introduced it on the Irish coast in 1804 in response to the Napoleonic Wars. At most of the signal stations a 'defensible guardhouse' or signal tower was erected, where the signal crew and military guard (to protect the signal crew) were housed. Signal towers were built to a standard design. They were generally of two storeys, square in plan and with a flat roof. The entrance doorway was at first-floor level, approached by ladder, and machicolations were placed directly over the doorway and over the landward corners of the tower. The flat roof was protected by a parapet incorporating the three machicolations. Most of the Cork signal towers were located within a rectangular enclosure with a semicircular or fan-shaped extension on the seaward side, where the signal mast was situated. From this position there was a view out to sea and along the coast in each direction to the next signal station, to which coded signals could be sent by hoisting balls and flags up the tall mast. In all, 81 signal stations were established at prominent locations around the coast, and at most of them a signal tower was erected, except for a few cases where the signal crew and military guard were accommodated in a fort, Martello tower or lighthouse. The signal stations were intended as a line of communication from Dublin to Bantry Bay and from Bantry around the west coast to Malin Head in Donegal. Many signal towers have survived, including a number on the coasts of Cork and Kerry, one on Hag's Head in County Clare, two on the Aran Islands and many on the Donegal coast.

*Signal tower at Carnlough, Blackball Head, Bantry Bay, Co. Cork. (Photograph courtesy of Colin Breen, Wes Forsythe and Rory Quinn)*

## SOUTERRAIN

AGE RANGE: EARLY MEDIEVAL

A souterrain is an underground man-made structure, consisting of one or more passages and chambers and usually with a narrow concealed entrance at ground level. They were used as temporary refuges in times of danger, and, being normally cool and dry, were also ideal storage areas for food. The vast majority are drystone-built with lintelled roofs, but sometimes they were cut into bedrock or hard boulder clay. A small number of examples built either partly or entirely of wood have also been found. Souterrains are rarely more than 20m or so in total length. The passages are generally about 1m wide and 1m high, and the chambers, which can be up to 2m high, are normally circular structures with corbelled roofs. Features of many souterrains are changes of level, which oblige the person entering to crawl while those further in can stand comfortably. This is clearly a defensive measure, so that an incoming attacker would be at a disadvantage. Another feature of souterrains is the unpredictable nature of their ground-plans. They frequently zigzag and twist, thus reducing the possibility of the occupants being dug out by raiders. A rare feature of souterrains is a hidden exit that served as an escape route for the people hiding inside. Souterrains are frequently found in locations associated with earthen or stone ringforts or associated with Early Christian ecclesiastical sites. Occasionally, however, they occur in isolation, independent of any known settlement sites. Over 3,000 souterrains have been found throughout Ireland, with concentrations in parts of counties Antrim, Down, Louth, Cork, Kerry, Galway and Sligo. *See also* **Ringfort**.

*A souterrain at Benagh, Co. Louth, looking from the chamber, out along the passage.*

## STANDING STONE

AGE RANGE: NEOLITHIC–MODERN (MAINLY BRONZE AGE)

The term 'standing stone' is usually limited to an otherwise featureless (without decoration or inscription) erect stone, also referred to as 'monolith', 'pillar stone', 'long stone', 'menhir' or by the Irish terms *gallán*, *dallán* or *líagán*. Standing stones were erected for various reasons at almost every period in time, not least as scratching-posts for cattle in recent centuries, but in prehistory they appear to have had a more symbolic meaning. Some standing stones were erected as burial-markers (for instance marking Bronze Age cist graves) or as commemorative monuments. Others may have acted as boundary-markers or route indicators. True prehistoric standing stones are unhewn and generally range in height from 1m to 5m. They are widely distributed throughout the country, with major concentrations in County Donegal, in the Iveragh and Dingle peninsulas of County Kerry and in west Cork. They are often prominent features of the landscape and are commonly located on hillslopes or towards the upper end of valleys. In counties Carlow and Kildare a group of granite monoliths occur around the edge of the Leinster Granite (e.g. Punchestown Standing Stone, Co. Kildare).

*One of a pair of standing stones at Baltray, Co. Louth. Evidence suggests that large structural stones used to build the Boyne Valley passage tombs were quarried at Clogherhead, Co. Louth. The megaliths could then have been transported by raft along the coast and up the River Boyne. If this was the case then this large standing stone, which was located very close to the then mouth of the Boyne, may have acted as a marker or route indicator for the tomb-builders. (Photo: P. Mulligan)*

## STAR-SHAPED FORT

AGE RANGE: LATE 16TH–17TH CENTURY

A star-shaped fort is an artillery fort whose wall projections give the ground-plan the shape of a star. Some of these forts are massive structures surrounded by dry moats and with pointed bastions on which cannons were mounted. They were built during the wars of the later 16th and 17th centuries, and some large examples were constructed to defend ports and towns. Duncannon Fort, Co. Wexford, for example, was constructed in 1588 to protect the estuary leading to Waterford Harbour against the expected arrival of the Spanish Armada. Charles Fort, Kinsale, Co. Cork, built in the late 17th century to protect Kinsale Harbour, is the largest star-shaped fortification ever built in Ireland.

*Charles Fort, Kinsale, Co. Cork. Built in the late 17th century, this star-shaped fort was designed to protect Kinsale Harbour. It is one of the largest military fortifications ever built in Ireland.*

## STONE CIRCLE

AGE RANGE: LATE NEOLITHIC–BRONZE AGE (MAINLY BRONZE AGE)

*Stone circle at Bohonagh, Co. Cork.*

Stone circles are arrangements of free-standing upright stones forming open rings, which were used for ritual, ceremonial and/or burial purposes mainly during the Bronze Age. Some circles have a large number of stones while the smallest ones have only five stones and measure just 2–4m across. One of the most impressive stone circles in Ireland is at Grange, Lough Gur, Co. Limerick, consisting of 113 stones surrounding an area over 45m in diameter. About 200 stone circle sites are known in Ireland, with two major concentrations in south Munster (Cork and south-west Kerry) and in mid-Ulster. In Cork and Kerry a distinctive form of stone circle is found. The entrance to these circles is through a pair of tall uprights, known as portals, and on the opposite side is a single 'recumbent' or 'axial' stone placed on its side rather than on end. The number of stones in these axial stone circles varies from nineteen to five, and the larger circles display a consistent orientation, with the axial stone normally being found on the south-west and the portals on the north-east of the circle. This consistent south-west/north-east orientation suggests some preoccupation with the position of the rising or setting sun. The second major concentration of stone circles is to be found in mid-Ulster, in counties Tyrone, Derry and east Fermanagh. These circles are different from the Cork and Kerry examples, often being of irregular plan and built of a greater number of quite small stones. In mid-Ulster stone circles often occur in groups and in association with stone alignments, as at Beaghmore, Co. Tyrone, where nine stone circles (many with associated stone alignments) were discovered beneath the surface of a bog. In addition to concentrations in south Munster and mid-Ulster, smaller groups of stone circles also occur at Lough Gur, Co. Limerick, at Cong, Co. Mayo, and in the west Wicklow/Kildare region. *See also* **Stone row**.

## STONE ROW

AGE RANGE: LATE NEOLITHIC–BRONZE AGE (MAINLY BRONZE AGE)

Stone rows (also called stone alignments) are alignments or straight lines of three or more closely set standing stones, erected to serve some ritual function. Three to six stones is the norm in stone rows in west Cork and in Kerry, where the rows are aligned along a general north-east/south-west axis and where many have the stones graded in height, with the tallest stone at either the eastern or western end. Apart from counties Cork and Kerry (where over 170 are known), stone alignments are also found in large numbers in mid-Ulster, where they are constructed of many closely set small stones and are often found in association with stone circles, as at Beaghmore, Co. Tyrone. *See also* **Stone circle**.

*Stone row at Maughanasilly, Co. Cork, dating from the Bronze Age.*

## SWEATHOUSE

AGE RANGE: POST-MEDIEVAL–MODERN (MAINLY 18TH–19TH CENTURY)

Sweathouses were erected from the 17th century onwards and were used for medicinal purposes in the treatment of various ailments, such as rheumatism. In some places they continued to be used right up until the late 1940s. In general they are small circular drystone structures, usually with a corbelled roof and usually built into banks or rising ground. The chamber inside (often with paved floor) normally ranges in height from 1.5m to 2m. The entrance is usually low and narrow, so that it can be blocked up easily. It seems that the sweating-cures took place mainly in the autumn. A turf fire was lit within the chamber and the house was heated for up to two days. Where turf was not locally available, wood, heather and brambles were used. After the fire had burnt out, the hot ashes were removed and the floor spread with bracken, grass or straw before the sweating took place. After the person or persons entered the house the entrance was sealed. In some cases water was poured onto the hot walls to create steam, but generally, it seems, they were more like saunas (dry heat) than Turkish baths. On emerging after a few hours, the patient would sometimes plunge into a nearby cold bath or stream. Sweathouses are invariably found in secluded places and are often sited close to streams. Although once widespread throughout the country, their present distribution is mainly in remote and depopulated parts of counties Leitrim (the county with the largest number of sweathouses) and Cavan, together with neighbouring parts of Roscommon, Fermanagh, Sligo and Donegal.

*Sweathouse, Doolargy, Cooley Peninsula, Co. Louth. (Photo: P. Mulligan)*

## TOWER HOUSE

AGE RANGE: LATE MEDIEVAL–POST-MEDIEVAL (MAINLY 15TH–EARLY 17TH CENTURY)

The tower house is the most common type of castle found in Ireland. They are tall stone towers, three, four or more storeys in height, and usually square or rectangular in plan. They were built as fortified private residences for affluent Anglo-Norman and Gaelic families during the period from about 1400 to about 1650. Tower houses are different from 13th-century keeps in that they generally cover a smaller ground area. Their masonry is not as massive and the entrance (a single door) is at ground level rather than at first-floor level. They usually have defensive features such as battlements protecting a wall-walk at roof level, a machicolation above the entrance, loops for archery or firearms, murder-holes inside the doorway, and narrow spiral stone stairwells. Also, as a defence against fire, one or more floors were vaulted in stone. Originally most tower houses had the extra protection of a defensive walled courtyard known as a bawn. In the 15th century numerous small tower houses were built in the Pale, as a result of a £10 grant to encourage landowners to build castles there. Over the stone-vaulted ground floor in these simple tower houses was a hall, and above that the private chambers of the owner. Most of the tower houses in the rest of the country date from the 16th century and are more complex, having more chambers and large fireplaces. At least 3,500 tower houses were originally built, particularly in the south and west of the country. Notable examples include Blarney Castle (Co. Cork), Bunratty Castle (Co. Clare), Aughnanure Castle (Co. Galway) and Ashtown Castle (Phoenix Park, Co. Dublin). Tower houses are represented on the Discovery Series maps by the term 'Castle'. *See also* **Castle**, **Bawn**, **Fortified house**.

## TUMULUS

AGE RANGE: NEOLITHIC–IRON AGE

A tumulus is a mound of earth heaped over a burial. It is usually circular in plan and can be 10m or more in diameter. There is no immediate visible source for the material of the mound, nor any evidence of a ditch or outer bank that might classify it as a form of barrow. On excavation, tumuli have been found to contain cist or pit burials, or simple pockets of cremated remains or even inhumations. Tumuli, like cairns, are usually situated on high ground. *See also* **Barrow, Cairn**.

*Aughnanure Castle, Oughterard, Co. Galway. Built in the 16th century, this is a particularly well-preserved example of an Irish tower house. Part of the corner turret of the inner bawn wall is visible to the left of the tower house.*

## WEDGE TOMB

AGE RANGE: LATE NEOLITHIC–EARLY BRONZE AGE (MAINLY EARLY BRONZE AGE)

Wedge tombs represent the last phase of the megalithic tomb tradition, being built between 2500 and 2000 BC approximately. A wedge tomb (also known as a 'wedge-shaped gallery grave') normally consists of a long, narrow burial chamber, which is generally broader and higher at the entrance and tapers in height and width towards the rear. Invariably the entrance faces in a westerly or south-westerly direction. Wedge tombs are roofed with slabs laid directly on the side walls, which often have one or more rows of outer walling. Evidence available from excavated tombs indicates that collective burial (both cremated and unburnt) was still practised by the wedge tomb-builders. Wedge tombs are the largest group of megalithic tombs in Ireland, with over 500 sites identified. The majority are located in the west of the country, with concentrations in counties Clare and Cork. They are found generally on light, well-drained soils rather than on the lowland drift-covered regions. They are represented on the Discovery Series maps by the term 'Megalithic Tomb'. *See also* **Megalithic tomb**.

*Wedge tomb at Altar, Co. Cork. The townland name is derived from this tomb, which was referred to in the past as an altar.*

## WINDMILL

AGE RANGE: MEDIEVAL–MODERN

The first recorded European wind-powered mills were built in Normandy, and it is probable that the Normans, after their invasion of Ireland in 1169, introduced windmill technology to this country. These early mills were wooden structures known as post mills, so called because the whole mill building was rotated about a central wooden post or pivot. The earliest recorded windmill in Ireland is thought to have been a post mill and was built around 1281 by the Anglo-Normans at Kilscanlan, near

*Restored small windmill, with thatched cap, at Tacumshin, Co. Wexford.*

*Restored four-sail windmill, Skerries, Co. Dublin. The thatched wooden cap rests on bearings and is turned to the wind, from inside the mill, by a hand lever. The earliest reference to a windmill at this site dates from the 16th century. (Photo: P. Mulligan)*

Old Ross, Co. Wexford. By the 15th century, however, post mills had been replaced by fixed tower mills, which were built of stone or brickwork. The tower mill was surmounted initially by a timber cap or roof, to which the sails were attached, and it was the cap alone, and not the whole structure, which was rotated (using a winch, fantail or tail-pole) so that the sails could face into the prevailing wind. Most windmills were built close to existing watermills and the miller used a combination of both to grind the corn. By the late 18th and early 19th centuries a number of technical advances were made in windmill construction. In 1745 a fantail wheel was introduced which allowed the cap to be automatically turned to the wind. Later, in 1760, the standard five-sailed windmill was introduced, and by 1783 a further 'shuttered' sail design greatly increased the windmill's operational efficiency. By 1800 windmill technology had reached its peak in Ireland, and in 1810 County Dublin alone had over 30 working windmills, all grinding corn for their local rural communities. As time went on, however, general industrialisation made the windmill obsolete, and by the end of the 19th century most of them had been abandoned. Examples of restored tower mills can be seen at Ballycopeland (Co. Down), Blennerville (Co. Kerry), Elphin (Co. Roscommon), Skerries (Co. Dublin) and Tacumshin (Co. Wexford).

# Translation of Irish words used to denote antiquities

| *Irish word* | *English translation* |
|---|---|
| *Barra* | Barrow |
| *Caiseal* (cashel*) | Stone-built ringfort, stone fort |
| *Caisleán* | Castle |
| *Carraig an aifrinn* | Mass rock |
| *Cathair* (caher*) | Stone-built ringfort, stone fort |
| *Cill* | Church |
| *Cillín* | Children's burial ground |
| *Cloch oghaim* | Ogham stone |
| *Clochán* (pl. *clocháin*) | Beehive hut |
| *Cosán* | Path, footpath |
| *Cosán na naomh* | Saint's path |
| *Crannóg* | Lake-dwelling, crannog |
| *Cros* | Cross |
| *Crosleac* | Cross-slab |
| *Daingean* | Stone fort, fortress |
| *Dallán* (pl. *dalláin*) | Standing stone |
| *Dún* | Fort, stone fort, fortress |
| *Dún cinn tíre* | Promontory fort |
| *Eaglais* | Church |
| *Fothrach* | Ruin |
| *Fulacht fia* (pl. *fulachtaí fia*) | Ancient cooking site ('deer roast'), burnt mound |
| *Gallán* (pl. *galláin*) | Standing stone |
| *Láthair Luathré Chríostaí* | Early Christian site |
| *Leacht* | Square drystone platform or altar |
| *Leachta cuimhne* | Memorial, commemorative monument |
| *Líne gallán* | Stone row |
| *Lios* | Earthen ringfort |
| *Mainistir Luathré Chríostaí* | Early Christian monastery |
| *Oileán daingnithe* | Fortified island |
| *Ráth* (rath*) | Earthen ringfort |
| *Reilig* | Burial ground, graveyard |
| *Séipéal* | Chapel, church |
| *Séipéilín* | Oratory |

| | |
|---|---|
| *Slí* | Way |
| *Snoíodóireacht chloiche* | Rock art |
| *Teampall* | Church |
| *Tobar beannaithe* | Holy well |
| *Tóchar* | Trackway (usually across a bog) |
| *Tuama meigiliteach* | Megalithic tomb |
| *Túr* | Tower |
| *Túr comhartha* | Signal tower |

(pl. = plural; * Anglicised version)

# GLOSSARY

**Antae**—A feature of a building where the side walls extend a short distance beyond the gable walls. Antae are found most commonly in churches built between the 10th and 12th centuries. It is assumed that they were structural features designed to support the roof.

**Bailey**—Fortified enclosed courtyard or ward surrounding or attached to a medieval castle. Also a fortified earthwork enclosure attached to a motte.

**Bartizan**—An overhanging turret supported on **corbels** and used defensively usually at the top corner of a building. Commonly found in tower houses and fortified houses.

**Bastion**—An outward projection from a defensive outer wall of a castle or fortress. Bastions are placed at corners or at intervals along the fortification in such a manner as to enable the defenders to direct flanking fire along the intervening stretches of wall.

**Battlements**—A **parapet** wall, divided into short solid portions (merlons) by regular openings (embrasures or crenels). Also called crenellation. 'Irish battlements' are a type peculiar to Irish fortifications where the merlons are stepped.

**Bellcote**—A small gabled or roofed housing for a bell.

**Chancel**—The east end of a church, where the altar is situated. The chancel is sometimes separated from the **nave** by a chancel arch. The chancel is normally reserved for the clergy and choir.

**Cloister**—A covered walk or arcade, often running round the sides of a quadrangle, with a wall on one side and a series of windows or an open colonnade on the other. Cloisters usually form part of the buildings of a monastery, convent, college or cathedral.

**Cloister garth**—An open space surrounded by a **cloister**.

**Corbel**—A stone projecting from a wall face and acting as a support to a wooden beam or to an oversailing course of stone or masonry.

**Corbelling**—The process of making a stone roof by laying courses of stone one on top of the other and overlapping inwards so that the gap is eventually narrowed and capable of being bridged by a single slab. The technique was used in Ireland to construct the roofs of some passage tomb chambers, souterrains, oratories and *clocháin*.

**Curtain wall**—The enclosing wall of a castle.

**Drystone**—Masonry constructed without mortar or clay.

**Fosse**—A ditch or trench of a defensive nature surrounding a defended or enclosed area. The material dug from the fosse would frequently be used to form a defensive bank.

**Gallery**—A subrectangular or wedge-shaped compartment in a megalithic tomb in which burials were deposited.

**Gothic**—A style of architecture characterised especially by the use of pointed arches and common from the late 12th century. The Cistercian order is credited with the introduction of this style of architecture to Ireland.

**Inhumation**—Burial of unburnt human remains.

**Jamb**—The straight sides of an archway, window or doorway.

**Keep**—The innermost stronghold or principal tower of a medieval castle, also known as a donjon. The keep is normally free-standing and situated in a fortified courtyard (**bailey**) surrounded by a strong **curtain wall**. In Ireland the majority of keeps are rectangular, but square, circular and polygonal versions also occur.

**Kerbstones**—A continuous line of stones at the base of a mound or cairn to keep it in place.

**Lintel**—A horizontal beam or stone placed over an entrance, a passage, a doorway or a window opening to support the weight above.

**Loop**—A narrow slit or opening in a wall, through which arrows or gunshot could be discharged. Commonly found in castles, tower houses and fortified houses.

**Machicolation**—A projecting **parapet** supported on **corbels**, with apertures in the floor through which rocks or hot liquids could be dropped on attackers. A feature of many castles and tower houses.

**Manor**—A self-sufficient landed estate or demesne, under the control of a lord who enjoyed a variety of rights over it and over the peasants (serfs) who worked on it. In Ireland, after the Anglo-Normans arrived, the newly conquered lands, in eastern parts of the country, were divided into estates known as manors.

**Moat**—A wide **fosse** or ditch, usually designed to hold water, serving as a defence or fortification.

**Mullion**—Vertical stone or timber dividing a window into two or more parts.

**Murder-hole**—An aperture in a floor or vault, usually above the main entrance passage to a castle or at the entrances to upper floors, through which intruders could be fired upon.

**Nave**—The main portion of a church west of the **chancel** and sometimes separated from it by a chancel arch. The nave is for the use of the congregation.

**Pale, the**—The district comprising parts of the modern counties of Louth, eastern Meath, Dublin and parts of Kildare, over which the crown of England held effective control in the later medieval period. It was, in part at least, delimited by a double ditch and bank.

**Palisade**—A fence of pointed wooden stakes, especially a feature of defensive works.

**Parapet**—A breast-high protective wall placed at the edge of a roof, platform or bridge. Parapets on castles are usually crenellated.

**Portcullis**—A gate of iron or wood, which was made to slide up and down in grooves, in the gateway of a castle.

**Rampart**—A defensive bank or wall surrounding a fortified place.

**Romanesque**—A style of architecture using the round arch in doorways, arches and windows, which was common in Ireland in the 12th century.

**Transept**—The transverse element of a cross-shaped church.

**Transom**—Horizontal bar of stone or wood dividing a window into two or more parts.

**Wall-walk**—A walkway positioned along the top of the roof and behind the **parapet** of a castle or church.

# References and further reading

Clinton, Mark (2001) *The souterrains of Ireland*. Bray. Wordwell.

Corlett, Christiaan (1999) *Antiquities of old Rathdown*. Bray. Wordwell.

Dúchas The Heritage Service (1986–2005) The County Archaeological Inventory Series. Dublin. The Stationery Office.

Flanagan, Laurence (1992) *A dictionary of Irish archaeology*. Dublin. Gill and Macmillan.

Harbison, Peter (1992) *Guide to national and historic monuments of Ireland*. Dublin. Gill and Macmillan.

Harbison, Peter (1994) *Pre-Christian Ireland*. London. Thames and Hudson.

Kerrigan, Paul (1995) *Castles and fortifications in Ireland 1485–1945*. Cork. The Collins Press.

Manning, Conleth (1991) *Irish field monuments*. Dublin. Stationery Office.

Manning, Conleth (1995) *Early Irish monasteries*. Dublin. Town House.

O'Keeffe, Tadhg (2000) *Medieval Ireland. An archaeology*. Stroud. Tempus Publishing.

O'Keeffe, Tadhg (2003) *Romanesque Ireland*. Dublin. Four Courts Press.

Ó Nualláin, Seán (1995) *Stone circles in Ireland*. Dublin. Town House.

O'Sullivan, Aidan (2000) *Crannógs: lake dwellings in early Ireland*. Dublin. Town House.

Rothery, Seán (1997) *A field guide to the buildings of Ireland*. Dublin. Lilliput Press.

Ryan, Michael (ed.) (1994) *Irish archaeology illustrated*. Dublin. Town House.

Stalley, Roger (1996) *Irish high crosses*. Dublin. Town House.

Stalley, Roger (2000) *Irish round towers*. Dublin. Town House.

Stout, Matthew (1997) *The Irish ringfort*. Dublin. Four Courts Press.

Sweetman, David (1999) *The medieval castles of Ireland*. Cork. The Collins Press.

Waddell, John (1998) *The prehistoric archaeology of Ireland*. Galway University Press.

# Index of place-names